THE GIFT

YOU DON'T HAVE TO FIGURE IT ALL OUT

VICKI BRAWNER

True Potential
REACH THE WORLD

THE GIFT
You don't have to figure it all out

Cover and Interior Page design by True Potential, Inc.

ISBN: 978-1-948794-02-2 (paperback)
ISBN: 978-1-948794-03-9 (ebook)
Library of Congress Control Number: 2018939491

True Potential, Inc.
PO Box 904, Travelers Rest, SC 29690
www.truepotentialmedia.com

Produced and Printed in the United States of America.

For you, Dear Reader:

May you step into true freedom in Christ.

"It is for freedom that Christ has set us free…"
– Galatians 5:1

Contents

Foreword

Vicki came into my life when she was eight years old, shortly after she and my daughter had become friends at school. A few years later I became her music teacher at that school. One day in her 5th grade year, she announced that she was going to travel the world singing for Jesus. I had the privilege of opening that door for her during her high school years when she began traveling the world with me as part of a singing group that went about sharing Jesus. And she has never stopped.

In this book Vicki addresses a struggle that is common throughout the Christian community. After accepting the gift of grace at the foot of the cross, she seemed to easily slip back into the pattern of trying to earn what had already been freely given. This, of course, is impossible. We have all learned early in life that circumstances are better for us when we perform well. This is true in family life, in school, in jobs, and in relationships. But as new beings in Christ, we are now told performing well is not necessary. Vicki's experiences and examples bring this dilemma close to home in our hearts. She doesn't stop there. In *The Gift*, she gives us scriptures and thoughtful insights into how to assimilate God's truths into our minds and hearts.

Those of us who are privileged to be in Vicki's life have seen her live out what she speaks. I testify to her qualifications to offer you the guidance that she has written in *The Gift*. She currently leads many teams on mission trips throughout the world for *In Motion Ministries*. We hear many reports about the impact she has had on the lives of these team members. She leads with genuine love and genuine life experiences that have taken her through the principles she shares with you in this book.

Having progressed from friend's mother, to teacher, to fellow minister and friend and now to colleague, I can truly say I have experienced life with Vicki. We've shared ups and downs, trials and triumphs. I feel personally qualified to encourage you to do more than just read *The Gift*. Soak it up. Thoughtfully go through the questions she asks. You will be blessed.

Norma Dunn
Founder and Mission Consultant
In Motion Ministries
www.inmotionministries.org

Acknowledgments

Many thanks to Marci Toler, my best friend and co-founder of *You Are Worthy Ministries*. God brought us together as we dug deep into His love for us. As iron sharpens iron, we have laughed, cried, discussed and challenged each other, growing in our understanding of His identity for us. To our team members Cindy Lundy and Saundra Dunn: you wonderful gals have inspired me and encouraged me to write these words. Thank you for your opinions and advice. It has been a pleasure exploring our *Identity in Christ* together on this journey.

I am so grateful to my sister, Debbie Unruh. You have been listening ear, first manuscript editor, loving critic, and the best cheerleader. I truly could not have completed this project without you.

My daughter Lauren Appelhans, who took my words, and with her editing talent, made them oh, so much better! You are a gift to me. I love you!

Norma Dunn: thank you for your kind words and your constant exhortation and encouragement. Most of all, thank you for believing in me completely—giving me so many opportunities to discover and put into practice God's calling on my life. Thank you for saying yes. Your yeses to Him opened the doors in my life. I will be forever grateful.

Seth Dunn, CEO of *In Motion Ministries*, lifelong friend and brother in the Lord: This book would not have happened if you hadn't led me to believe it was possible. Thank you for pushing me when I need it, and for standing strong when I need someone to lean on. You believed I could fly when I didn't believe I had wings. Here's to many more years of reaching the nations with the goodness and love of our incredible Father.

To Steve Spillman, founder and president of True Potential Publishing, Inc., and Daniel Barrozo, editor: Thanks so much for your excitement in this project. You have been such an encouragement and so easy to work with. I appreciate all your hard work; you have truly blessed me.

To my husband and children: your love and support touch me beyond words. I love you.

Foremost, I want to praise and thank the Lord, the lover of my soul and the very breath I breathe: Thank You for gently teaching me of Yourself and sharing with me Your wisdom, Your insight, and Your compassion. It is You Who holds me together, and all my love is Yours.

Vicki

Introduction

Her calendar is full. She has projects due at work. She gets a message from a friend to meet at a coffee shop for some "catch up" time. There's that thing on the back burner that she really needs to have time to process with her husband … appointments to keep, church responsibilities, chores to do at home … she has a sister going through a difficult time … she has a dream to go and do and be…

She needs a few moments just to think. To pray. To feel. But if she begins to feel, what will happen? Maybe she's not measuring up to all the expectations. There's a lot of pressure—what if she stops for a moment and someone discovers she's barely hanging on? That she *wants* to be the perfect wife, mother, and colleague, intimately walking with Jesus and getting through each day winning—but that feels beyond her reach?

Do you know this woman? Is she familiar to you?

There's a place deep inside each of us that wants to be loved. Truly loved. Accepted. Understood.

I'd like to invite you on a journey—let's discover who you are in the eyes of the Lover of your soul. The One who knows you inside and out, and celebrates *you*.

As a busy wife, mother of five, minister, missions planner, missionary, writer, and musician, I'm just a gal who has juggled and tried to balance all the pressures of life while seeking meaning and integrity in my 'everyday.' I have asked many times, "Who am I? And does it matter?" Discovering the reality of how my Creator views me has changed everything.

The Gift is a 6-week workbook for women, in groups or individually, who want to find peace and rest in the chaos of our busy world. We can't always change the circumstances or the conditions in which we live, but when we step into the reality of who we were created to be, our inner-life can be enveloped and energized by peaceful confidence and wholeness.

Grab a cup of coffee, your Bible, and a pen. Gather your friends, and let's discover your true identity together.

You Are Worthy Ministries is a non-denominational, non-profit Christian ministry that seeks to share the truth of our identity in Christ—leading women into the freedom of the New Covenant and leaving behind the bindings of performance, shame, and unworthiness.

We believe our Identity in Christ provided through the New Covenant will change women, families, communities, and the world. It is our desire that everyone associated with *You Are Worthy Ministries* experience the intense emotion of connecting with God and His amazing love for us. From this desire, we provide Christ-centered, high-quality, purpose-driven seminars and retreats for women that create lasting impact.

You Are Worthy Ministries is a branch of In Motion Ministries, a gateway to the mission field—providing education, training, and worldwide opportunities to minister God's love.

Vicki Brawner

Visit us at:
www.youareworthyministries.org
www.inmotionministries.org

CHAPTER 1

YOU ARE WORTHY

Does the title of this first chapter stop you in your tracks? No, then *really* think about it: "You are worthy."

Many times, we hear positive phrases we are "supposed" to believe about ourselves, and even sometimes, we agree with them to some extent—but actually living them is another story altogether. My heart is filled with compassion for the women I meet who are struggling with their true identity in Christ because all this positivity simply sounds like great words, not reality.

If I were sitting with you at a coffee shop, and we were having a heart-to-heart, I could compliment you on your outfit, or that you always seem to have it together, and that I love your smile. While I would be sincere and truly mean every word, you may smile kindly and respond with a heartfelt "Thank you," but something deep inside you would just put all those words in a box labeled "Don't Believe It." We could continue our conversation, touching on all the things going on in our lives, what is keeping us busy, and maybe even how we feel about those things. But…something is missing, isn't it? Wouldn't it be nice to actually *believe* the things I said about you — from a place of not just confidence, but *really* knowing it in your "knower"? Because you AGREE with me? Never from an arrogant, self-absorbed ego, but from the understanding of how Jesus sees you at all times (not just when you've done it right) and walking in the freedom this brings?

Many of us lost something shortly after the initial "joy of our salvation" wore off. When we came to a saving knowledge of Jesus Christ, accepting His tremendous sacrifice for our sins, we were elated. Relieved. So very thankful. Definitely in awe of Him and this love we were feeling. Somewhere along the way, however, somebody told us we had to "live right," be a "good Christian," "display the right attitude" and get busy doing good works. Please hear me when I say that none of these things are bad or wrong. But somewhere along the path of attempting to please the One to whom we were so grateful and trying to obey the commandments, we lost our joy and fell into a trap of carrying our own burdens and trying to undo the things for which we have felt guilty. Somewhere, false humility told us we really aren't "all that," and we need to spend our time keeping things clean and tidy – not just outside, but inside too. We began to live in the land of "should." You know, this stressful place inside our heads where all we can hear is "You should be more understanding," and "You should give more time, money, energy, help, etc., at church," or "You shouldn't feel that way. It's not godly." This dark *Valley of Should* is a scary place to be because it is continuously robbing us of peace and contentment. Many of us are carrying a too-heavy load of tasks and responsibilities that we were never designed to carry.

What if your "Don't Believe It" box was filled not with supposedly undeserved compliments, but rather the lies from the enemy of our souls? That the lovely things said to you and about you are things you can agree with because you are standing in a place of grace and know that Jesus' character is shining through you so, of course, they are true?

Can you imagine the freedom you would feel if you believed the Lover of your soul is not mad at you, is not expecting you to toe the line, and is actually thrilled with you just the way you are…right now?

Sisters, I invite you on a journey. Let's discover who you are in the eyes of Father God, Jesus Christ, and Holy Spirit. He is filled with joy when He thinks of you, when He sees you, when He dreams of you. "You are altogether beautiful, my darling; there is no flaw in you" (Song of Songs 4:7, NIV).

GROUP TALK:

1. Have you ever felt that you don't measure up to the standards of a "good Christian"? Why or why not?

   _____

   _____

   _____

   _____

   _____

   _____

   _____

   _____

2. How do you feel when asked, "What if you didn't have to figure it all out?"

   _____

   _____

   _____

   _____

   _____

   _____

   _____

   _____

CHAPTER 2
TRUTH

Let's take a look at where this freedom really comes from, and how we can truly walk in all He offers us.

After God created the earth and people to inhabit it, there was a disaster to the relationship He designed. Ephesians 1 tells us that before the foundations of the world, we were *in* Him. He craved relationship and created us to be in right relationship with Him for all eternity. God's enemy became jealous and as is his nature, sought to steal, kill, and destroy that beautiful communion (John 10:10). God, in His infinite grace, put a plan in place to restore the relationship with His beloved creation and defeat His enemy forever. He sent His son, the perfect representation for mankind, who was sinless, to take on the sins of the world for all time—past, present, and future—and pay the debt. He purchased a new identity for all who believe and trust in Christ's *finished* work on that cross. He died and was resurrected to *new life* by the power of Holy Spirit. This same Spirit resides in you and me, empowering us to walk in His grace, which is His ability working *in* us.

In the beginning, after the relationship between God and man was severed, He began to work His plan of restoration starting with Abraham; one He loved very much. He made a covenant with Abraham promising that anyone born into Abraham's lineage would be blessed with the right to inherit all of God's promises. If they carried Abraham's blood, they were blessed abundantly—not because of the way they behaved, but because they had the right *lineage*. As Abraham's descendants began to populate the earth, God was pleased to heap blessings and acceptance upon them—all because they had the right pedigree and happened to be born right. He did not punish or turn His face away from them when they behaved against God's character of love, honesty, and truth. He turned a blind eye to their ugly behavior and continued to take care of them as long as they had the blood of Abraham flowing through their veins.

For example, it is frustrating to read about Abraham's lie that his wife was actually his sister, so he could give her away to be raped by Pharaoh—just to save his own skin! God did not punish Abraham for this misdeed; although, He did punish Pharaoh for his transgression against His chosen ones, Abraham and Sarah. Why didn't God care if Abraham lied and let his wife endure a horrible situation? We ask this because of our mindset that comes from the next covenant that God made with Moses. This mindset still influences the way we think. We don't relate to the idea of pedigree being enough to protect anyone from the wrath of God. We do relate to the idea of trying to live right. Abraham and his descendants did many more things we would consider deserving of punishment and death, but God just continued to bless them anyway because His promise of the right pedigree was true. We call this promise the Abrahamic Covenant.

At the time of Moses, a descendant of Abraham, God was still at work aiming toward restoring relationship. He blessed His people, the Israelites, delivered them from the hand of slavery, and continued to give them His presence and provision. All this *even* when they griped and complained and were so ungrateful. He then asked them all to gather at the base of Mt. Sinai, prepared and purified, because He wanted to be present with them, speaking to them through Moses (Exodus 19). Again, He desired relationship with His creation. As Moses prepared the people for worship, God in His powerful presence descended from the mountain and spoke to them through thunder, lightning, and smoke, giving them His commandments on how to live in relationship with Him and one another. They were all standing at a distance in fear of such a powerful God. They were so afraid that they asked Moses to get the commandments from God *for* them. So God proceeded to give Moses His laws and rules for living—all the ways to live a holy life before Him.

Now the people would be held to a higher standard of performance-based behavior; failure to adhere to this standard was met with sudden and drastic punishment.

They now had to earn what they previously possessed through birthright. What a shock! We need to understand that this law was given to show them—and us—the need for a Savior. It is impossible to keep all these laws and rules. It is impossible to hold to this high standard of performance. At that time, failure to meet this standard resulted in His withholding of presence and provision; His anger poured out on them. We call this mandate the Mosaic Covenant.

> "What was once reserved for Abraham's enemies and foreigners to God's promises, was now poured upon Abraham's descendants who failed to adhere to the conditions of this law-keeping covenant." (*He Qualifies You*, Mansbridge, pg. 39.)

> "But now God has shown us a way to be right with Him without keeping the requirements of the law, as was promised in the writings of Moses and the prophets long ago. We are made right with God by placing our faith in Jesus Christ. And this is true for everyone who believes, no matter who we are." (Romans 3:20–22, NLT)

God was still making a way to restore the relationship for which we were designed. His son Jesus said, "Don't misunderstand why I have come. I did not come to abolish the law of Moses or the writings of the prophets. No, I came to accomplish its purpose" (Matthew 5:17, NLT).

Jesus—who had the perfect pedigree, the right lineage—was sinless and kept all the law perfectly. *He* was the perfect representation of the Abrahamic Covenant and the Mosaic Covenant. He was the only One of all time who could take our place. He exchanged that perfect life for ours. He *became* sin for us (2 Corinthians 5:21), taking all the punishment we deserved, paying the price for us to be back in relationship with Holy God.

This New Covenant is an agreement between Father God and Son Jesus and is not based on birthright or behavior. Jesus accomplished all that, saying, "It is finished." Until this point, the presence of the Lord was contained in a section of the temple called the Holy of Holies. Only once a year was anyone allowed to be in His tangible presence, and that was only permitted to the High Priest. God's presence was separated from the people by a very thick curtain in the temple. The Old Covenant era ended when this curtain was ripped in two the moment Jesus was killed, paying the cost for all sin for all time. Now His presence resides with us and in us, through His Holy Spirit. This was accomplished through Jesus' death and resurrection.

Now all of God's promises are available to us—not because of our birth or lineage, not because of our performance, but because our belief in Jesus places us *in* Him who has the pedigree and who accomplished the performance to perfection. Because that beautiful exchange of His life for ours took place, we are now able to live as a new creation *in* Him (2 Corinthians 5:17). We become co-heirs with Christ, giving us the full rights of sonship—we get to walk in His presence and provision. This frees us from having to earn His love. We no longer must perform to be perfected. It is all HIS work, and NONE of our own.

This new identity says, "You ARE Worthy." Why? Because before the foundations of the earth, you were *in* Him (Ephesians 1:4). He chose you to be *in* Him, so you are worthy because *He* is worthy. You don't have to possess the kind of faith Abraham had, or be born in the right bloodline, or keep all the laws and rules—this new life is a free gift to you if you only believe.

What does this New Identity do for us?

- Removes all need to perform. You are accepted no matter what.

- Removes all guilt and shame. In fact, these two feelings are "illegal" in a New Covenant mindset—He took it all. This means they are not part of your DNA as a new creation and have no place as you walk in your new identity.

Let me introduce you to my best friend Marci and her story.

My story…Where do I begin? Where do I end?

I guess I begin with this…my family, every one of us, are high achievers. We are second generation Americans, growing up on the stories of hard work, responsibility, expectation, and family reputation. My grandfather immigrated to America, going through Ellis Island twice, just to make sure he was really staying. He homesteaded in Western Nebraska and expected his children to secure and live the American dream. My family has college degrees and most have either a postgraduate degree or a professional licensure. All great goals and dreams. I often joke, my family can turn nearly anything and everything into a competition: from executing the best tube run behind the boat, to card games, to more serious concerns about diamond sizes, cars, a house's square footage. You get the idea…We perform.

We don't necessarily attempt to *be* the best in our family, but we certainly feel the need to *do* our best, with the total expectation that our best should be better than average. We feel we cannot disappoint the "family."

I have yet to reconcile this expectation to "good" or "bad' parenting or family issues. I just know that it shaped how I saw God and my relationship with Jesus Christ. I saw our Father God as a stern judge—visualize the Lincoln Memorial. He was sitting in His Kingdom and on His throne...

Watching…

Waiting…

Smiling when I was doing well…

Frowning when I was not doing all that well.

For far too many years, I didn't even know I had it wrong. I just attempted to perform, thinking if I was performing well, I was making my family proud. Of course, that meant that God was well pleased. I mean, He gave me these gifts; shouldn't I be responsible to use them to handle the things placed in front of me? If I was tired, I just wasn't managing my time well. I needed to dig deeper and keep going. If I was failing to achieve the next promotion, I just wasn't enough. If my husband wasn't happy, it was something I failed to do.

I was very busy performing. I was keeping the house, making the meals, working, raising kids—not to mention I was also an Army Reserve officer, taking command, leading soldiers, going off to war…

I was really busy, performing…

And then I failed.

My marriage failed.

I failed to get promoted.

I was even failing at managing my team.

Okay, I get it…My children were fine, I was alive and relatively healthy, but my identity was destroyed. I had no idea who I was. I had no idea how Father could love and cherish me…I had failed. I was a failure.

And then, I heard something that changed everything. It was a translation of Genesis 3:8, "But the Lord God called to the man"—but what I heard was, "God pursued them." Wait… What? God pursued them. He looked for them. He sought them out? That means that He left the throne and looked for them. So if He left the throne to look for Adam and Eve, is it possible that He is pursuing me? Is it possible that I just have to stop running, stop staying so busy that I cannot rest, stop running to perform? Is it possible that if I just stop for a moment, and turn around, God the Father of the Universe is right there, pursuing me? If that is possible, is it possible that I might, just maybe, be Worthy of His Love, just because?

I honestly had to ruminate on this idea for a while. I had to examine this idea from a logical approach and from an emotional approach. It changed everything!

As I came to accept this idea, I also examined the purpose and meaning of the New Covenant of Christ Jesus. I was taking into my head and my heart His death and resurrection—not just learning the words. His living sacrifice to end one covenant and enter into a totally new covenant with our Father, on our behalf. Christ

Jesus ended the rule of law, the performance period of our history. The Father and Son love us so, so, so much that they changed the rules that we can be in community with them. No one else did anything—it was a sacrifice and commitment between the Father and the Son, an act that God already knew and planned. You and I do not have to do anything; we are gifted this relationship. Even more, there is no performance, no effort, no standard that I can achieve or not achieve to change the rules...so I do not have to perform to be loved. I am simply loved.

I am enough. I am complete. I am worthy.

Do you find yourself reacting to the idea that you may be living your life in "performance mode"? After all, we have been told most of our lives to "plan your work and work you plan." Early on, we were constantly asked, "What do you want to be when you grow up?" Then our culture conditioned us to perform at the highest level possible, accompanied by the pressure to achieve. "And what's wrong with that?" you might ask. "How else would I ever accomplish anything?"

When we come to a saving knowledge of Jesus Christ, when we realize His great love and sacrifice for us, we come running with open arms and are so grateful for His salvation. For many of us, however, the ingrained patterns of performance continue to shape our lives, and we believe the lie that "It is your responsibility to figure it all out; you should live right, act right, and love right."

Soon we have fallen back into performance mode and believe it is up to us to prove ourselves acceptable. Sadly, we carry this burden into our relationships and careers, all the while being told to "Be the best!," "Aim for the top!" and "Do it right!" We forget that Jesus did it all, and He invites you into His performance—this means freedom for you.

Do you walk around carrying a load of guilt? A load of "shoulds"?—"I should…but I don't" or "I can't." Ugh. That feels heavy. Jesus said, "My burden is light and easy." We only need to carry His light. Not guilt. Not shame. He desires to heal the broken places in you that are not displaying the New Identity for which He paid a very high price. His work was enough. We don't need to help Him carry our load. It's not our responsibility. It doesn't make us look better to others if we take responsibility for our pain and shame. He paid for it. We mustn't carry it—if we try, it tells Him that His work was not enough.

He invites you into the position of being *IN* Him, walking in His steps, letting Him think His thoughts in you. He heals and restores the broken places and calls you by a new name (Revelation 2:17).

Let's review:

1. Abrahamic Covenant: the people of God were accepted through pedigree—birthright, lineage, bloodline. As long as they carried the blood of Abraham in their veins, they were in right standing with God.

2. Mosaic Covenant: now the requirement to keep the law is added to their pedigree. What they *do* is as important as who they are. When they can't meet the standard, punishment is death. Romans 6:23: "For the wages of sin is death, but the gift of God is eternal life through Jesus Christ our Lord." This covenant demands correct performance with severe consequences for disobedience.

3. New Covenant: Jesus fulfills all requirements of the two previous covenants. He exchanged His perfection for our imperfection, giving us a New Identity.

This is not to say the first two covenants were somehow "bad" or "wrong." They held a very important place in the plan of Father to restore humankind back to right relationship with Him. We, in this time and place in history, must understand where we fit into this divine plan and live according to the grace given us by the incredible sacrifice and finished work of Christ on the cross—the third covenant. We then get confused when we try to live according to the previous covenants. Sadly, the enemy, our culture, and human nature have taught us to live in "mixed covenant" theology, and we cannot measure up to the standards we somehow believe are put upon us. The freedom Jesus purchased for us is ours to walk in the life He exemplified, and He provides all the grace and ability to do so.

GROUP TALK:

1. Before reading this chapter, did you understand the three covenants and that they are separate?

   _____

   _____

   _____

   _____

   _____

   _____

2. In what areas of your life do you find yourself "performing" to please God or people?

   _____

   _____

   _____

   _____

   _____

   _____

3. If you removed the burden of performance, how would your life be different?

   _____

   _____

   _____

   _____

   _____

   _____

SCRIPTURES TO STUDY:

- Ephesians 1:3–14, Jeremiah 1:5

  _____
  _____
  _____

- Abrahamic Covenant: Genesis 12–50 (from Abraham to Joseph)

  o Key passages: Genesis 12:2–3, 17:6–7

  _____
  _____
  _____

- Mosaic Covenant: Exodus 19, 20:1–21, 24

  _____
  _____
  _____

- New Covenant: Matthew 5:17, Romans 8:31–39, Colossians 2:9–10, 1 Corinthians 6:17, Romans 6:6, Galatians 3:27–28

  _____
  _____
  _____

For more study on the Three Covenants, read _He Qualifies You_ by Chad Mansbridge.

CHAPTER 3
HOPE

Jesus says,

> *"Anyone with ears to hear must listen to the Spirit and understand what He is saying to the churches. To everyone who is victorious I will give some of the manna that has been hidden away in heaven. And I will give to each one a white stone, and on that stone will be engraved* **a new name** *that no one understands except the one who receives it."*
> (Revelation 2:17, NLT, bold emphasis mine)

Let me tell you a story:

I was raised in a loving, God-fearing home; I learned about Jesus as a toddler. My family was part of a religious denomination that seeks to follow Jesus, but it focused on a set of rules and regulations to keep a person acceptable in the Lord's eyes. This mindset caused pride to be one of the "big" sins—and we were to avoid doing anything that could set us up to fall into that trap. As a child, I was encouraged to build my strengths, but never look for compliments. In fact, it was better to downplay any recognition and never appear to be bragging or arrogant. This "sin of pride" drove fear into me; I felt I would have the worst kind of punishment and shame if I was ever caught feeling proud of my looks or accomplishments.

I have heard it said that the question in every woman's heart is "Am I beautiful?" This was definitely true for me, and I was desperate to hear the answer "YES!" The problem was that all the compliments or criticisms came through this filter: the fear of pride staking its claim in my heart, ultimately proving that I was unforgivable and unacceptable. I believed my worth and value would be determined by how I believed or reacted to the opinions of others towards me. The criticisms were exaggerated in my mind as I heaped guilt and condemnation upon myself, always willing to believe anything negative spoken about my appearance, my abilities, or my character. The compliments were thrown away, never to be believed. In fact, I thought it better to contradict them with the "truth" of my imperfections in case anyone—especially myself—should see me in a positive light. This false humility was upheld as a good "Christian virtue," telling me that the more I hated myself, the more acceptable I would be to Holy God and those with whom I had relationship.

I had no idea that throughout my childhood, adolescence, and young adult life I had built very tall, strong walls around my heart. I was trapped inside these walls, searching for the answer to my question. This lie shaped my existence. When I was criticized, bullied, or shamed, these found their way through the cracks, and I believed them as truth. When I was built-up, complimented, or affirmed, these bounced off the brick walls or were thrown back over the top as quickly as possible.

I'm sure you can imagine what kind of damage this does to a young woman looking to get married and start a family. I brought my woundedness into my marriage, continuing to soak up all criticism and negative words and actions as only a person like me "should deserve." I married someone who carried his own wounds and unsatisfied questions of identity, causing the two of us to go down a very painful path. Sadly, this marriage took the worst kind of hit, and we could not survive the damage.

I continued down the road of seeking the answer to my question, limping and broken; I was still trapped, but inside even thicker walls. I was now facing it alone with the responsibility of raising five children. It was at this place in my journey that Jesus reached through the walls and began to teach me of Himself. He is so tender and compassionate. He knew exactly how to handle my deeply wounded heart. He began to speak to me about my true identity, the one for which He paid such a high price. He showed me through Scripture, through books, and through relationships that I am indeed a New Creation

(2 Corinthians 5:17), and that He desires to live *HIS* life in me (Galatians 2:20).

Before the foundations of the earth, He thought of me, designed me; He says I was in Him (Ephesians 1:4). He did a beautiful exchange—my ugly, wounded pride-filled life for His pure, victorious, joy-filled one. Oh, the relief I felt as the guilt and shame rolled off me! I no longer had to carry the load of responsibility for performing to the standards I had believed were required. His life was a free gift, and it was easy and light to carry—and I got to lay down my HUGE burden.

His love and unconditional acceptance began to tear down my walls, one brick at a time. I was no longer trudging this journey alone as I had believed. He brought me deep relationships and a supportive community. As the bricks came down, the words of affirmation began to leak in. I began to hope that someday I would actually believe them!

Jesus ministered forgiveness to my trampled heart in such a tender and gracious way. He showed me that unforgiveness is like drinking poison and expecting the other person to die. What? Had I slowly been killing myself as I held grudges and disappointment against all the people in my life who had wounded me? My unforgiveness was not punishing them as I had hoped, but it was slowly sapping the life out of me and causing me to wither away. What freedom there is in forgiveness!

As I released each person I had held responsible, as I began to pray for them and allow Jesus' kindness and love for them to permeate my deepest soul, I began to walk in healing and wholeness. His life and energy broke down more of the wall and brought the Springtime green of a new life, delivering me from the bonds that trapped me in that hideous prison.

His compassion filled me so much that I began to see the people who had caused me pain in life the way He sees them—as beloved. No longer did I hold them responsible for my pain because pain ultimately comes from the enemy of my soul, and I was walking hand-in-hand with the Lover of my soul. Soon, the walls were crashing down with great force as I was released from the dark prison of self-loathing, hatred, and unforgiveness. Oh, how bright the sunshine is when there are no more shadows!

It is interesting to note that throughout the Old Testament, when the Israelites were required to bring a sacrifice to atone for or cover over their sin, God required a perfect animal for that sacrifice—one without spot or blemish. We are no longer under the Mosaic Covenant, and animal sacrifices are no longer required because Jesus' sacrifice was the perfect one that God required—Jesus willingly took our place, that beautiful exchange.

Romans 12:1 says, "And so, my dear brothers, I plead with you to give your bodies to God because of all He has done for you. Let them be *a living and holy sacrifice*—the kind He will find acceptable. This is truly the way to worship Him" (NLT, emphasis mine). I am discovering that just as in the Old Covenant, God requires perfection for the sacrifices offered to Him—and that Jesus was that perfect sacrifice taking our place. In that exchange, He traded His life for ours, now making you and me a New Creation; He heals and restores all the wounded places in our hearts. This now allows us to offer a healed, whole sacrifice–living on that altar for His glory. We get to walk in victory, living the life He provides, allowing Him to think His thoughts in us, speak His words through our lips, love with His love everyone around us.

One of the amazing things His sacrifice paid for is the grace to walk in belief of all the things that belong to this new identity. It's one thing to learn this, quite another to truly believe it. As He began to speak to me of beauty, He brought another husband into my life. Every day this amazing guy tells me I am beautiful. What a tremendous blessing! But my ability to believe it was still broken. So once again, Jesus tenderly met me at that place and ministered His grace–which is His ability in me. Although I was learning it was His life in me that makes me acceptable, I found myself unable to accept myself. I could graciously thank people for their compliments, no longer throwing them away, but I could not truly believe them yet.

I started this chapter with Revelation 2:17. Jesus says, "Whoever has ears, let them hear what the Spirit says to the churches. To the one who is victorious, I will give some of the hidden manna. I will also give that person a white stone with *a new name on it*, known only to the one who receives it" (NIV, emphasis mine).

So I began to ask Jesus what my name is. I asked Him this question for a couple of years. He led me down a path of discovery, speaking to me of all the victories in which my new identity allowed me to walk.

Many, many times I would ask, "What do you call me?"

While I was teaching at a leadership conference one day, and unbeknownst to me, one of my co-workers—and precious sister in Christ—was asking Holy Spirit what He thinks of me. She loves to minister to people in this way, sharing with them what she hears the Lord saying, encouraging and giving them value. She had no knowledge of this private conversation I was having with Father. She wrote down what she heard Him say on a note card. When I came into the conference room and found my seat, it was sitting on my notebook. "He says, 'I call her Bella.'" Bella means beautiful. He answered my question–in the deepest part of my soul. He calls me Beautiful! Somehow, He reached into the deepest part if my soul and birthed in me the ability to believe Him. His supernatural power touched me and, in a split second, I believed. My dear friend had no idea that writing a few words on a card she'd heard Him speak would destroy the last of the walls that had surrounded my heart. He is so good.

You, too, probably have that deep part of your soul that you desire for Him to touch—to hear Him speak to you with His soft, gentle voice. Ask Him, "What do you call me?"

As you discover His answer, I believe it will answer many of the deep-seated questions that only you and He knows you are asking. "If you believe, you will receive whatever you ask for in prayer" (Matthew 21:22, NIV).

He truly desires to answer your question "Who am I?" He invites you into intimate relationship, where He meets all your needs and answers the hard questions. If you will spend time with Him, opening all the closed-off rooms in your heart, He will delight in exposing the darkness with His light—leading you to a place of truly walking in your new Identity in Christ.

GROUP TALK:

1. How would you describe "Intimate relationship" with God?

_____

_____

_____

_____

_____

_____

_____

2. Do you have this relationship with Him?

_____

_____

_____

_____

_____

_____

_____

3. Spend some time asking God what HE thinks about you. Write down what you hear Him say.

_____

_____

_____

_____

_____

_____

4. Ask Him, "What do You call me?" Write down what you hear Him say.

_____

_____

_____

_____

_____

_____

_____

SCRIPTURES TO STUDY:

- Revelation 2:17

  _____

  _____

  _____

  _____

- 2 Corinthians 5:17

  _____

  _____

  _____

  _____

- Romans 5

  _____

  _____

  _____

  _____

  _____

- Romans 7:4–6

  _____

  _____

  _____

  _____

- Romans 8:9–11

_____

_____

_____

_____

_____

- John 10:3–5

_____

_____

_____

_____

_____

- Psalm 46:10

_____

_____

_____

_____

_____

CHAPTER 4

DREAM

A deep search is going on inside all of us–a hole that we desperately want filled. We have been created with a yearning to be cherished and the ability to walk confidently in the person we were designed to be.

Can you begin to imagine the possibilities–the reality of stepping into your authentic self? What if you could truly embrace your new name, stand in belief of what HE says about you, dare to dream the dream HE holds for you?

Several years ago, Marci and I both signed up for a "Biggest Loser" program at our local gym. This is actually how we met—we were placed on the same BL team. We were determined to drop as many pounds as possible in a short amount of time. We had no idea that Father was actually inviting us on a life-changing journey to discover the reality of discovering our New Identity.

Our desire to lose weight stemmed from a deeper heart condition, but we were focused on the tangible issues on the surface. We both arrived to the first meeting in determined "performance mode." *We thought, We can do anything for three months. Just power through and we will get the desired results!*

We definitely performed! Our trainer became exasperated with our level of competition and performance. She had to constantly redesign our workouts because we were NOT going to fail; no one on the team could out-work us! We ended the three months of being constantly sore with the frustration of little weight loss and feeling like failures.

The Lord, in His great mercy, began to chip away at our hearts, showing us that performance and strength were not going to bring about the dream in our hearts. We both foolishly thought that weight loss would answer the questions in our hearts: Marci's "Am I good enough?" My "Am I beautiful?"

The deeper desire–that is actually God-breathed–was to be who we were created to be. To step into believing what HE says about us as truth, walking in the confidence of this identity.

As we began the journey of discovering this identity, He showed us that our worthiness comes from *His* performance, and we no longer have to walk in fear of others' opinions or our own condemnation.

Believing what He says about you brings you to a place of following your heart with the energy it takes to accomplish it.

What "huge thing" is calling you? The one thing that seems impossible? The one that is so big but fundamental that you have no way of accomplishing it by yourself?

Understanding who you are allows you to imagine it and then to walk there. Let Him peel back the layers of surface answers and look deep inside. He has specifically designed you and called you into *HIS* dream for you.

The answers to these questions come as you spend time with Jesus in the secret place, in communicating with Him on an intimate level. As you dialogue with Him, He will show you the grand possibilities that are behind the nuggets of desire that you spend your time thinking about and wishing for. Grab ahold of the nuggets, knowing that He will lead you to the greatness behind them–remembering that HE is the One at work to bring it to completion.

> *"And I am certain the God, who began a good work in you will continue His work until it is finally finished…"* (Philippians 1:6, NLT)

I believe we find ourselves saying to God, "Just tell me what I'm supposed to do, and I will do it." This is backwards thinking and slams us right back into "performance mode." We must first believe that what HE says about us is true, and trust Him. Out of that trust, we must take the first step. He will provide the steps that follow. It is not ours to "figure it all out."

I have never read a Bible story that made logical sense.

For instance, God told Abraham to pack up all he owned—which was quite extensive—and go. Go where? God did not draw him a map and a five-year plan. He said, "…go to the land I will show you" (Genesis 12:1, NLT). Who does that? But Abraham trusted and obeyed.

God told Joshua to send His people to walk around an enemy city–one time every day for six days. On the seventh day, they were to walk around the city seven times and then shout. What kind of battle plan is that? Not a logical one!

He told Hosea to love and marry a prostitute who would continue to leave him and cheat on him–and to take her back every time. Does this make sense?

Jesus found some fishermen hard at work, told them to drop their nets and follow Him–then took them on a three-year journey. Is this responsible?

If logic, responsibility, and the need to see the whole plan nags at you, lay that down at His feet and choose to trust Him. What He says about you *IS* true. You ARE worthy because of His life given to you. It may not look logical, but He thought it and designed you for it.

If we know this truth and hear our new name, we can show up authentically to the way He sees our life unfolding. We must accept the truth that He sees "the amazing version of me"–live into the possibility of this dream.

Responsibility says, "Plan."

Dreams say, "Step and trust."

Are you chasing the results of figuring it all out? Lay that down and step into your identity. The result will turn out to be what He is calling and creating in you.

Just when Marci and I were chasing change on the surface to bring about the desired results of confidence and beauty, the Lover of our souls instead invited us on a journey of discovery. As He spoke to our individual hearts of the potential He saw in us, we began to ask Him to show us His dream. We began to see that weight loss was not the concern, but the fact that He cares if we show up authentically to His eye view of us. Does He care about how I take care of my body? Absolutely. But we were trying to get our identity questions answered by performing work on the surface, and He wanted to show us what He truly sees.

What are you doing to get your questions answered? Oh, how He desires to show you what He sees when He looks at you. He calls you by name and invites you to step into His dream for you.

GROUP TALK:

1. What is the dream you have in your heart?

    _____

    _____

    _____

    _____

    _____

    _____

2. List the things on your current "plan."

    _____

    _____

    _____

    _____

    _____

    _____

3. What does it look like to "step and trust" in these things?

    _____

    _____

    _____

    _____

    _____

    _____

SCRIPTURES TO STUDY:

- 2 Corinthians 5:7

  _____
  _____
  _____
  _____

- Philippians 1:6

  _____
  _____
  _____
  _____
  _____

- Romans 8:30

  _____
  _____
  _____
  _____
  _____

- Romans 11:29

  _____
  _____
  _____
  _____

- Ephesians 4:1

  _____

  _____

  _____

  _____

  _____

  _____

- 2 Thessalonians 1:11–12

  _____

  _____

  _____

  _____

  _____

  _____

CHAPTER 5
FREEDOM

One of the things I am learning about Holy Spirit is that He teaches me a concept, gets me all jazzed and passionate about it, and then I begin telling everyone around me of this new learning. Only after letting it permeate my mind, He draws me into a place of teaching my heart the true concept through my circumstances. There is such a difference between head knowledge and heart knowledge. I can tell you all day long that you were not designed to figure everything out; you were designed to walk by faith and trust in His ability to provide it all. We can discuss this, think of biblical examples, and have a wonderful verbal encouragement session, walking away from our conversation feeling great—and then walk right into circumstances that put all those wonderful words and concepts to the test.

As I write this chapter, I am tempted to worry about all the things in my life that are overwhelming me. It seems there are never enough hours in the day to accomplish all the tasks and assignments clawing for my attention.

Juggling my family and home responsibilities, my job, my relationships, my dreams and goals—it's all too much, and I am always stretched to the limit of my ability to control it all. *Any 'Amens'?*

Who told us we have to figure it all out? Society? The 'American Way'? The Bible?

Stop what you are doing and think of the three most pressing worries on your mind and heart.

Not too difficult, right? I'm sure they are very close to the surface.

I have a question for you: What if you didn't HAVE to figure it all out?

What would the next hour, the next day, and the next week look like if you did NOT have to figure it all out?

The next month?

The next year?

We have all been raised to start planning our lives as young as five or six years old with the question, "What do you want to be when you grow up?"

Somewhere along the way, we were told it was our responsibility to "plan your work and work your plan."

Sayings like "God helps those who help themselves," which is totally unscriptural, by the way, "The early bird gets the worm," "Don't put off till tomorrow what you can do today" have shaped many of our early lives. They have taught us to rely on ourselves and our own planning and decision-making ability to "get 'er done."

This has cultivated a culture of stress and worry, self-reliance, and a huge set-up for failure. The pressure that comes with the push to figure it all out can be crippling.

It causes us to carry a gigantic load–one we were not designed to carry.

Look with me at Philippians 4:6 (NLT), where we have been given some direction–a formula–that produces the answers for which we are looking:

"Do not worry about anything…"

Wait.

Stop right there.

REALLY?!

Didn't Apostle Paul understand this feels impossible? Who doesn't worry, after all? Worry is so normal that we dismiss these words "as unrealistic" and pretend this verse is "not talking to me."

"…pray about everything…"

You say, "I am! All the time!" Right? "OH, GOD! What do I do about X, Y and Z?" Then we begin to worry… and plan…and stress out…and try to figure it out.

"…tell God what you need…"

Does He really care about my details? We all need something. Surely He doesn't need to be bothered by my stress—there are hurricanes in Haiti, famine in Africa, people dying in floods, and crime running rampant on the streets.

Who am I to bother Him about the latest fight with my kids or gas for my car? Does He really care that I don't have the energy to face today? My problems can look so little in the grand scheme of things—but they are overwhelming to me!

"…and thank Him for what He has done…"

Where have you seen Him meet a need in your life? Did He come through *because* of your worry and your ability to figure it out? You know what I'm talking about, that time when one of your problems was resolved in a way you could never have imagined.

He doesn't need us to "help" Him solve all our issues by spending our energy on worrying.

As we begin to thank Him for who He is, what He has done, how He has held us together—the stress begins to dissipate. This almost feels too easy, right?

Is it really a formula?

The next words are "…then you will experience God's peace, which exceeds anything we can understand" (verse 7). Isn't this what we are craving? When worry and stress eats us up, all we want is for peace to calm our weary souls.

He said:

1. Don't worry
2. Pray about it, telling Him what you need
3. Thank Him

    1+2+3=PEACE…that is incomprehensible!

There is nothing in this Scripture that tells me to make a plan, get it all together, figure it out.

EVEN IF I caused the issue in the first place!

He is serious about this. In the Bible He tells us 365 times, "Do not fear." That's one for every day of the year! Worry, stress, and the pressure to "figure it all out" are all based in fear. The fear of failure, of unsatisfactory results, of disappointment, of loss. There is NO fear in love. He IS LOVE.

He can hold you together. He DOES hold you together. His desire and delight is in taking care of you and all you need.

Verse 19 says,

> *"And this same God who takes care of me* **will supply all your needs** *from His glorious riches, which have been given to us in Christ Jesus."* (Bold emphasis mine)

He's not too busy for your details. Nothing is too big or small for His attention in your life. He does NOT require you to figure it all out.

I know it is true. As I write this chapter, Father is proving to me that He meant what He said.

For example, my daughters and I had been invited on a mission trip to South America. This was all very exciting, and we were focused on all the wonderful things that will happen in this opportunity: Lives changed, the Kingdom expanded as we share the gospel, the growth in ourselves that we know happens to team members on an adventure like this. At the back of my mind—okay, SCREAMING to the *front* of my mind—was the huge amount of money required for four of us to step into this dream. My bank account is already stretched to the max in raising my family; I cannot just write a check for the more than $8,000 that it costs for us to go. My biggest temptation right at this time? Worry.

How would we raise that much money? Where in the world will it come from? What can we do to make this happen?

As my mind jumped from peace and excitement to worry and fret, I heard the gentle whisper, "What if you didn't have to figure it all out? Will you trust Me?"

"Yes, Lord, I will. I will take the steps YOU put in front of me and not try to jump ahead and figure out how this will come about. Show me the first step."

Martin Luther King, Jr. said, "Faith is taking the first step even though you can't see the whole staircase."

God is faithful. As I constantly–what seemed like hundreds of times a day—put my worries and fears in His hands, and took the steps He gave me, there was an unexplainable peace and confidence in my heart. With each passing day of trust, the peace got more real, and we could focus on preparing for the trip.

I then got an email saying we had been fully funded for this mission! When I asked how it happened, the answer surprised me. There was no possible way I could ever have figured out how to raise the money from the sources God used to provide! People from all over had sent in money, completely unbeknownst to me.

He does not work within the scope of our limited understanding. When we place each concern in His capable hands, and truly, truly leave it there, He provides in ways we cannot imagine.

I have been watching the Lord teach this to Marci. He is so good! Her 30-year career is coming to a close, so naturally she has been concerned about her future. How will she provide for her family and all of her needs? Each day as the temptation to worry and try to figure it all out overwhelms her, she has asked Father to take care of it. She is learning to truly trust and to expect Him to do what He says.

He showed her the first step of starting a new business. This, of course, brings with it many opportunities to worry. As the options to worry and fret or to trust come up in her life daily, she is placing each one in His hands, saying, "What if I didn't have to figure it all out?" Super difficult for a planner who likes everything lined out! Father continuously rewards her simple trust with blowing her mind as He provides new clients from places where she has never even advertised!

I'll share one more example from my personal journey. Eight years ago, our family experienced a tragedy. Through it my seventeen-year-old son walked away from us and our home. This estrangement was completely unexpected and devastating. No words can describe the grief that overwhelmed me as each new day dawned, and he was not at the table eating meals with us. He was not in the living room hanging out with us. I didn't hear his voice talking to his sisters or hear him playing his guitar. He wasn't playing his favorite video games.

Talk about worrying! How does a mother place pain and anxiety into the Lord's hands and leave it there, trusting that the One who holds her together will also restore the broken? Minute by aching minute I had to make the conscious choice to let Him take care of my son—and take care of the next five minutes…tomorrow…next week…and beyond.

As I cried and prayed, the Lord would instill deep within me the ability to trust Him. That's what grace is—*HIS* ability in me. As the minutes turned into days, the days into weeks and months, and yes, into years, He continued to provide the ability to trust the whole situation into His hands. He did not expect me to drum up the ability myself. *HE* is the provider. Not just of physical provisions but of things like the ability to believe and trust, the ability to forgive, the compassion to see things from another's point of view—not just my own.

As I put into practice this lifestyle of minute-by-minute trusting, it truly became a habit. In no way could I have tried to figure out how to restore a broken relationship. But the Lord paid a huge price to heal our wounds, to bind up the broken-hearted, to make crooked paths straight. There is such unexplainable peace when you open your clenched fists that are gripping all your worries tightly. He is so very capable of not only holding those anxieties but of holding *you* together. Every one of your details matters greatly to Him.

"My grace is all you need. My power works best in weakness" (2 Corinthians 12:9, NLT). Grace = His ability. It is enough. Always.

As I continued to pray, trust, and yes, shed tears, time continued to march on. The Lord delivered peace to me that kept me rising in the morning to face another victorious day of living in hope.

About three years after the incident, my son began to acknowledge me. Ever so slowly. I would reach out to him on his birthday, and he would respond. Months would go by, and we would invite him to a holiday family gathering. He began to timidly attend, each time staying a little longer. With every step, I would rejoice–and cry– and praise the Lord for His faithfulness. Many months later, I remember receiving a hug from him. Oh, it had been so long since I was able to wrap my arms around my child. He was quickly growing into a man, and I was grieving the loss of experiencing his "firsts" of young adult life. Yet, Holy Spirit would whisper to me, "I am here with him, and with you. Trust Me, and rejoice in the baby steps of restoration that you are experiencing." Again, *trust*.

In the last 6 months, my son has chosen to make bigger strides towards me and come back into relationship. Now we can have hugs, conversations, and mutual respect for each other. The awkwardness is dissipating and every time we are in each other's presence, the relationship is being restored in greater measure. God is *so* faithful! Worry, anxiety, and trying to figure it all out would never bring about my desire of being in beautiful relationship with my son. Trust, and the ability provided by the Lover of my soul, brings about the healing and restoration that is unimaginable!

So, what if you didn't have to figure it all out?

How would that change your minute-to-minute life? Your stress level? Your relationships? The way you communicate and effect everyone around you?

Those three things that are on your heart—the ones at the beginning of this chapter—open your hand and heart, releasing them into the Lord's hands. Let Him take care of you.

HE WILL FIGURE IT ALL OUT.

GROUP TALK:

Stepping into all that God has for you is easy when you understand who you are–because He *always* provides for everything *He* dreams about you.

1. What are the three things asked for in this chapter?

   _____

   _____

   _____

   _____

   _____

   _____

   _____

   _____

2. What is holding you back from your dreams?

   _____

   _____

   _____

   _____

   _____

   _____

   _____

   _____

   _____

   _____

3. List what happens to the things holding you back when you put them through the Philippians 4:6 process: 1+2+3=PEACE.

_____

_____

_____

_____

_____

_____

_____

_____

_____

_____

4. What could you be if/when you see yourself as He sees you: *in* Christ, with your needs fulfilled?

_____

_____

_____

_____

_____

_____

_____

_____

_____

_____

_____

5. Ask yourself, "What if I didn't *have* to figure it all out?" What does this look like in your daily decisions?

_____

_____

_____

_____

_____

_____

_____

_____

_____

_____

_____

_____

SCRIPTURES TO STUDY:

- Philippians 4:6–8

  _____

  _____

  _____

  _____

  _____

- 2 Corinthians 12:9

  _____

  _____

  _____

  _____

  _____

- Psalm 94:19

  _____

  _____

  _____

  _____

- Proverbs 3:5–6

  _____

  _____

  _____

  _____

- Matthew 6:25–27

_____

_____

_____

_____

_____

_____

- Matthew 6:34

_____

_____

_____

_____

_____

_____

- Philippians 4:19

_____

_____

_____

_____

_____

_____

CHAPTER 6

RELEASE

"Give all your worries and cares to God, for He cares for you." (1 Peter 5:7, NLT)

What are you done with? Are there things you are carrying around in your "backpack" that you would like to be done with?

Maybe it's the need to perform. Have you been working hard to do it all "right"? Has life pressured you to the point of breaking, feeling you just can't measure up to whatever standard is in front of you?

Ladies, let's put down the backpack. Isaiah 41:13 says, "For I hold you by your right hand—I, the Lord, your God. And I say to you, 'Don't be afraid. I am here to help you'" (NLT).

Maybe your pack is filled with grief. Have you worn sadness so long it has become too familiar, like your favorite sweatshirt? "He has sent Me...to comfort all who mourn...to give them beauty for ashes, the oil of joy for mourning, the garment of praise for the spirit of heaviness" (Isaiah 61:3, NKJV). As you take off that sweatshirt, let Him clothe you with joy.

Maybe you're like me, and you have felt unnoticed and ugly. Song of Songs 4:7 says, "You are altogether beautiful, my darling. There is no flaw in you" (NLT). Let Him speak this to you. He truly delights in you and sees you as absolutely gorgeous!

Lay down the shame. The guilt. You are not allowed to carry these anymore. It is illegal in the Kingdom point of view. The King paid for it. He took it. You may not claim it back as something you must carry. If you insist on carrying even just a little shame, you are essentially telling him that "Your work was really not enough for me. I need to help carry it...to do my part."

Ladies, His work was and *is* enough.

He took it ALL.

He carried everything.

In exchange for your pack filled with pain, heaviness, and despair, He clothes you in white and calls you "Beautiful."

YOU ARE WORTHY!

Now that you are laying it down, and determining in your heart not to pick it up again, let's bask in the peace of this moment. Do you feel the weight come off your shoulders? Can you breathe easier?

Take a look with me at this ancient story told in John 4 about the woman at the well. Let's look at it through the eyes of identity and letting go.

The chapter opens with Jesus and His disciples trekking back to Galilee from Judea because the Pharisees are giving Him trouble. They have to cross through Samaria, a part of the country that holds a lot of tension. The Jews and the Samaritans have a long-standing disagreement, and the pain runs deep. Normally, if a Jew needed to make this journey, he would go the long way around just to avoid the trouble he might encounter and also to keep himself "clean" from the assumed filth of what he might term "the half-breeds." This judging, selfish, and arrogant behavior on both sides made for an animosity that was contrary to the message Jesus was living and spreading.

Jesus becomes weary from His travels and sits down to rest at a well while the disciples go into town to buy food. It is the middle of the day—hot and sultry—and He is feeling thirsty.

A woman comes to the well, carrying her jars to fetch water for her daily needs. This is a strange time for her to be doing this since it was customary for the women of the village to gather early in the morning while it was still cool. They would come to socialize and start their day with all the latest news and gossip of the village happenings. This particular woman, we will call her Photina, was not welcome to come at the normal time for water drawing because she had been branded as a sinner and an outcast by her peers. *It is always amazing to me how we can be so cruel to one another.* Coming alone at noon, the hottest part of the day, was far more preferable than hearing once again the names called to her and the disgusted looks thrown her way.

As she approaches the well, she is startled to see a Jewish man sitting there. I can imagine her trying to think of a way to avoid an encounter…was it possible to escape without Him noticing her?

Just as she is scrambling for a quick retreat, He does the unthinkable.

He speaks to her.

"Will you give me a drink?"

Uh-oh. Immediately she is on the defensive. Photina cannot comprehend why a Jew would be talking to her, a Samaritan woman, an outcast at that. You can hear the years of heartache in her response.

"You are a Jew, and I am a Samaritan woman. How can you ask me for a drink?"

She is incredulous. Why? In our modern culture of equality and hyper-sensitivity to roles and gender, we don't understand the enormity of this situation. The culture of that day had steadfast rules:

1. Jews weren't supposed to speak to Samaritans.
2. Men weren't permitted to address women without their husbands present.
3. Rabbis had no business speaking to shady ladies like this one.

Jesus was willing to toss out the rules, but Photina wasn't. Those rules and her culture and ethnicity defined her.

Jesus immediately answers her question with a confusing statement.

"If you knew the gift of God and Who it is that asks you for a drink, you would have asked Him and He would have given you living water."

Photina is like the rest of us and is so caught up in her physical circumstances that when He speaks to her on a spiritual level, she is flabbergasted and has no grid to process it. The term 'living water' in that day and place referred to a live spring, probably because it looks 'alive' when the water bubbles out. Is this man daft? This is a *well*, not a spring! Can you hear her thinking, *What does living water have to do with anything here at this well? And besides the fact that He is talking to me without my husband here, He has nothing to hold the water. Oh, what am I to do?*

As she points out that Jesus has nothing to draw water with, she remembers He mentioned something about knowing *who* He was. Curiosity gets the better of her and she asks, "Are you greater than our forefather Jacob, who gave us this well and drank out of it himself?" She is still thinking and acting in the physical realm. So, Jesus bridges the gap. He tells her of the eternal life He is offering anyone who wants it, comparing it to the living water that comes out of a spring, but this water will quench the deep thirst of their souls with only one drink.

Photina now begins to grasp that He is different and offering her something amazing. But she still can think only on the immediate and physical level. Water that will quench her thirst forever? How awesome would that be if she never had to come to this horrible well in the heat of the day again to avoid all the hate and anxiety she faces every day? Who wouldn't want that?

Jesus' heart of compassion sees her desperate desire for freedom and knows just how to show her who she *really* is. He cuts right to the quick, bringing up the most painful subject in her life.

"Go call your husband and come back."

Can you relate to the panic that must have risen within her at that moment? Photina has spent every day doing what it takes to deaden the pain of the choices she has made—or maybe were made for her—and has lived her life trying to avoid the ugliness that seems to claw at her identity. We still do the same thing today—

carrying our secret burdens of shame, hoping we have hidden them well, nobody noticing. If they are too noticeable, we avoid the people and situations where they will be displayed for all to see. Jesus wants to touch those things and bring them to light because He loves and fully accepts and heals.

I imagine the look on Photina's face—the shutdown of emotion and the deadness in her voice as she replies, "I have no husband." She feels like everything He just said and the hope she had of some relief from her anguish was no longer available. After all, she doesn't deserve it. As she straightens her back and steels her nerves, she determines to do whatever it takes to get this encounter over with.

Jesus surprises her once again with His response. "You are right. You have no husband. In fact, you've had *five* husbands—and you are not married to the one you are living with now. Yep, you are right."

What?! How does this man know my secrets? He must be a prophet. The only thing she can think of to end this conversation is to go back to the age-old fight of Jew versus Samaritan. Maybe if she can get Him all riled up about the normal things the two rivals fight about, she will get out of there and it will be over. As she brings up a hot topic of territorial rights between the two nations, He once again diffuses it with speaking of truth—never taking sides.

So she says dismissively, "I know that the Messiah is coming. He can explain everything to us."

Just as Photina is thinking she can get out of this weird and awkward situation, Jesus blows her mind one last time and tells her who He really is. "I, the one you are talking to—I am He." In this moment, He reveals himself, and she understands all that He has been saying. He fills her with belief and joy.

It is at this place, at the well situated in the hot and dusty road, that Photina lays down all that she has been carrying. He gives her, in exchange, that new life He has been talking about. A drink of that living water that flows into all the places that were shriveled and dried up, washing away all the hurt, the filth, and the despair. Her new identity is "Beloved." All the names, the regret, the shame—now exchanged for acceptance, honor, and beauty.

This new identity carries with it freedom, boldness, and the ability that up to this point was impossible. She runs to the village where she has only known heartache and defeat, and with joy tells everyone of *Him*.

Can you imagine what the people in town were thinking? What has happened to her? The change was not only recognizable, but obvious for all to see. She urged them all to come to Jesus, and they did! They came to see Him. He gave them the same offering of living water, and many in that town believed, even asking Jesus and the disciples to stay with them. He continued to talk with them, even more coming into the Kingdom.

How easy would it have been for Jesus to enter the village, begin preaching in the street, touching people, healing them, and giving them new life? After all, He had been doing that all over the country. But Jesus wanted Photina to see who she really was, not what she had been called, not what she believed about herself. He wanted her to step into her true identity—the one He calls all of us into.

The change in her was so dramatic that an entire village was brought to Jesus. Photina let go of all she was carrying and was free to step into all He had for her.

What about you? What would you like to lay down at the well and leave there, so you can step into who you really are?

If you take an honest look into your "backpack," what do you see that you have been carrying that is not in your New Identity? The names you have been called, the experiences that have shaped you, which you thought belonged to you, so you must "buck up" and carry?

Let's sit next to Jesus at the well and empty the backpack, exchanging our wounds for His healing Living Water.

GROUP TALK:

1. Are you ready to exchange your worries for your New Identity?

    _____

    _____

    _____

    _____

    _____

    _____

2. If so, what are you laying down?

    _____

    _____

    _____

    _____

    _____

    _____

3. What are you picking up and wearing as your New Identity?

    _____

    _____

    _____

    _____

    _____

    _____

SCRIPTURES TO STUDY:

- 1 Peter 5:7

  _____

  _____

  _____

  _____

  _____

  _____

- Isaiah 41:13

  _____

  _____

  _____

  _____

  _____

  _____

  _____

- John 4:1–42

  _____

  _____

  _____

  _____

  _____

  _____

  _____

- Colossians 3:2

_____

_____

_____

_____

_____

_____

- Psalm 62:8

_____

_____

_____

_____

_____

_____

CHAPTER 7

NEW BEGINNINGS

Stepping into all that God desires for us requires seeing ourselves from His point of view. Our position in Him, in the New Covenant, allows us to be much more than most of us can comprehend. The work Jesus did on the cross for us, the *finished* work, did not just pay for our sins and give us eternal life. It really is oh, so much more.

The word salvation is *sozo* in Greek. It means: Deliverance, Preservation, Soundness, Prosperity, Happiness, Rescue, General Well Being, Safety, Liberation, Release, Forgiveness, Healing, and Restoration.

Do you see how this knowledge can be transformational in our everyday lives? Yes, Jesus paid a high price to restore our relationship with Him, so we could spend eternity in heaven with Him—love without end. But, more than that, He also exchanged His life for ours—on earth as it is in heaven. We get to walk with Him here, as He walks in us, and experience and be all that is true in heaven. Kingdom living is about operating in the profound love God has for us and displaying all the attributes of *sozo* (salvation) to everyone we meet.

You will begin to notice as you walk with your backpack lightened and emptied of all the things you laid at the well, people around you will see a difference in you. What an exciting time to share with them all you are discovering as you operate in your New Identity.

A profound peace surrounds people who walk in their True Identity, and it seems to be a magnet of God's grace to others. You will notice people asking you why you look different and appear so peaceful. Take these God-given opportunities to invite them on this incredible journey of discovering who they truly are and how they are viewed from Heaven's eyes.

I find it important to have reminders around me of this New Identity I walk in. If you are like me, you will be going along just fine, and your circumstances will present an opportunity either to walk in this grace or to react in the way you were accustomed before you understood who you truly are. It is at these times that a reminder is a wonderful way to confirm in your heart what you know is true. Then make decisions and act accordingly.

Let me give you an example. My sister has chosen a reminder song—one that many of us are familiar with from childhood—"Jesus loves me, this I know." We have heard and sung these words often, but they hold so much truth. On the days when she is tempted to believe she is unlovable, that no one really cares, that loneliness and darkness are the only things defining her existence, she consciously makes an effort to sing this simple tune. As the truth of it sinks in, she is reminding herself of the truth Jesus has spoken to her: "You are loved beyond compare. You matter. I am delighted in you. You are mine. I love you." These words of life and truth can change the atmosphere in the blink of an eye and cause her to walk in the reality of who she is.

I encourage you to take some time with Jesus and ask Him for a verse, a song, a picture, something you can use as an anchor to remind yourself of who you truly are. Fully Accepted. Treasured. Loved beyond compare. Called. Honored.

Sisters, let's take a minute to rejoice and reflect on the incredible gift He has given us—His life in exchange for ours—that we might walk in freedom!

THANK YOU JESUS!

GROUP TALK:

1. Describe yourself in the words He says about you.

   _____

   _____

   _____

   _____

   _____

   _____

2. Look up verses that confirm who you are in Him.
   List them here.

   _____

   _____

   _____

   _____

   _____

   _____

   _____

3. Which "anchors" or "reminders" do you want to
   keep handy to keep walking in the truth of your
   New Identity?

   _____

   _____

   _____

   _____

   _____

   _____

Let us pray

My Dear Jesus,

Thank you for my sisters who are on this journey of discovering who they are in You. I ask that You take each one by the hand and by the heart, showing them exactly what You think of them. Lead them to that intimate place where You hold their hearts, where You hold them together, where You speak tenderly to them. As You call them each by name, teach them their value. As they grasp the truth, bring others alongside them who can begin the journey too. Thank You for Your deep love and the life you breathe in us. Amen.

About the Author

Vicki Brawner is a wife, a mother of five, a singer/songwriter, an ordained minister and co-founder and director of *You Are Worthy Ministries*. She has served as a missionary in Costa Rica, as a short term mission trip leader to more than 30 countries, and as a youth leader for her church. Her journey includes the heartbreak of divorce, the struggles of single motherhood, the joy of remarriage, and the assurance of living in a real, daily relationship with God. She is filled with compassion for those struggling to see themselves as Jesus sees them and gently invites them into the journey of discovery and acceptance of their true identity.

youareworthyministries.org

inmotionministries.org

My personal Facebook ministry page:

facebook.com/VickiSmithBrawnerIMM

Instagram: **Vicki Smith Brawner_IMM**

Women's ministry Facebook page:

facebook.com/YouAreWorthyMinistries.Org

Notes:_____

_____

_____

_____

_____

_____

_____

_____

_____

_____

_____

_____

_____

_____

_____

_____

_____

_____

_____

_____

_____

_____

_____

_____

_____

_____

_____

_____

_____

_____

_____

_____

_____

_____

_____

_____

_____

_____

_____

_____

_____

_____

_____

_____

_____

_____

_____

_____

_____

_____

_____

_____

Notes:_____

_____

_____

_____

_____

_____

_____

_____

_____

_____

_____

_____

_____

_____

_____

_____

_____

_____

_____

_____

_____

_____

_____

_____

Notes:_____

_____

_____

_____

_____

_____

_____

_____

_____

_____

_____

_____

_____

_____

_____

_____

_____

_____

_____

_____

_____

_____

_____

_____

_____

_____

_____

Notes:_____

_____

_____

_____

_____

_____

_____

_____

_____

_____

_____

_____

_____

_____

_____

_____

_____

_____

_____

_____

_____

_____

_____

_____

_____

_____

_____

_____

_____

Notes:_____

_____

_____

_____

_____

_____

_____

_____

_____

_____

_____

_____

_____

_____

_____

_____

_____

_____

_____

_____

_____

_____

_____

_____

_____

_____

_____

_____

_____

_____

_____

_____

_____

_____

_____

_____

_____

_____

_____

_____

_____

_____

_____

_____

_____

_____

_____

_____

Notes:_____

_____
_____
_____
_____
_____
_____
_____
_____
_____
_____
_____
_____
_____
_____
_____
_____
_____
_____
_____
_____
_____
_____
_____
_____
_____
_____
_____

_____

_____

_____

_____

_____

_____

_____

_____

_____

_____

_____

_____

_____

_____

_____

_____

_____

_____

_____

_____

_____

_____

_____

_____

_____

_____

_____

Notes:_____

_____

_____

_____

_____

_____

_____

_____

_____

_____

_____

_____

_____

_____

_____

_____

_____

_____

_____

_____

_____

_____

_____

_____

_____

www.ingramcontent.com/pod-product-compliance
Lightning Source LLC
La Vergne TN
LVHW051810080426
835513LV00017B/1896